DODD, MEAD WONDERS BOOKS

Wonders of Herbs

SIGMUND A. LAVINE

Illustrated with photographs

Coriander Seed

DODD, MEAD & COMPANY • NEW YORK

For ROSEMARY—
in remembrance of all the rue I've caused her

Illustrations courtesy of: American Spice Trade Association, 3, 7, 13, 21 *top*, 22, 36, 40 *bottom*, 61; Brooklyn Botanic Garden, Philip B. Mullan, 23 *bottom*; W. Atlee Burpee Company, 2, 6 *bottom left*, 8, 9 *left*, 10, 11, 12, 16, 17, 18, 20, 24, 25, 28 *bottom*, 32 *top*, 44 *left*, 59 *top*, 62 *bottom*; Durkee Famous Foods, 21 *bottom*; R. T. French Company, 34 *top*, 63; Jane O'Regan, 15, 23 *top* (after Dydymus Montaine, *The Gardener's Labyrinth*), 28 *top*, 31, 33, 34 *bottom left*, 43 *right*, 44 *right*, 48 *right*, 55 *top center and top right and bottom*, 60; Park Seed Company, 45 *bottom*, 62 *top*; Vincent Scuro, 26; United States Department of Agriculture, 6 *except bottom left*, 9 *right*, 29, 30, 32 *bottom*, 34 *bottom right*, 35, 38, 40 *top*, 43 *left*, 45 *top*, 48 *left*, 51, 55 *top left*, 59 *bottom*.

Frontispiece: *Coriander, popular cooking herb*

Library of Congress Cataloging in Publication Data

Lavine, Sigmund A
    Wonders of herbs.

    Includes index.
    SUMMARY: Discusses the history of herbs, their culti-
vation indoors and out, individual herb facts and lore,
and their use today in beauty aids.
    1.   Herbs—Juvenile literature.   2.   Herb gardening—
Juvenile literature.   3.   Herbs (in religion, folk-lore,
etc.)—Juvenile literature.   [1. Herbs]   I.   Title.
SB351.H5L3   635'.7   75–38356
ISBN 0–396–07294–1

Contents

Ginger

Paprika

Foxglove, source of digitalis

Leaves and berries of black pepper

Celery seeds

1
The History of Herbs

Parsley

"That which we call a rose . . ."

Herbs have played an important part in the history of man from prehistoric times to the present. Over the centuries, peoples throughout the world have used herbs as amulets, condiments, dyes, incense, love philters, medicine, perfume, in religious ceremonies, and as charms against witchcraft. Herbs have also been employed to fashion wreaths to crown victorious athletes and as wedding and funeral decorations. In the days when windows were rarely opened because of the stench of open sewers, herbs were strewn on the floors of both public buildings and private homes to freshen the air. Meanwhile, practically every culture has amassed a vast store of legends and superstitions dealing with herbs.

WHAT IS AN HERB?

Strangely enough, although "the history of herbs is, indeed, a history of mankind itself," there is no standard definition of the word "herb." Botanists—students of plants—consider any vegetation with soft, succulent tissue an herb. Actually this definition is not satisfactory. While it is true that many herbs lack hard tissue (at least above the ground), those species that evolve into shrubs or trees have woody trunks. Moreover, cer-

7

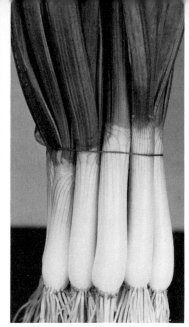

Vegetables that are herbs—onions, rhubarb, and scallions

tain herbs have woody stems. Still other herbs develop woody tissue as they grow older. But the majority of herbs have soft stems that die down to the ground seasonally, the roots remaining alive and producing new growth year after year in the way of all perennial plants. On the other hand, some herbs are annuals and die completely each year. While a number of herbs reseed themselves, others must be replanted by man.

Because of the many exceptions to the botanical rule that classifies various plants as herbs, some authorities ignore the technical meaning of "herb" when talking to, or writing for, the general public. But even these individuals cannot agree on a simple definition of an herb. Some consider any useful plant an herb. Others limit herbs to wild or domesticated vegetation that man either eats or uses to flavor, preserve, or season food. These experts also classify plants that have medicinal value or furnish materials for cosmetics as herbs. But any plants used for one or more of these purposes are commonly called herbs by the average person.

8

Because of its sweet odor, woodruff was often strewn on floors to sweeten the air during the Middle Ages.

Garlic—an herb strong in flavor and favor

HERB FAMILIES

Most herbs are members of three large plant families: Umbelliferae, Compositae, and Labiate. The list that follows includes some of the best-known species in each of these groups.

UMBELLIFERAE	COMPOSITAE	LABIATE
angelica	camomile	balm
caraway	chicory	basil
chervil	dandelion	catnip
coriander	endive	horehound
dill	lettuce	lavender
fennel	tarragon	oregano
parsley		peppermint
		rosemary
		sage
		spearmint
		summer savory
		sweet marjoram

9

Every part of caraway has value but the greatest use is made of its seeds, which were utilized by cooks in ancient Egypt.

The majority of the Umbelliferae are pleasantly scented and the oils extracted from these aromatic species have long been employed to conceal the bitter taste or disagreeable odor of certain medicines. But far greater use is made of these fragrant plants in cooking than in the manufacture of pharmaceuticals.

Although some herbs belonging to the Compositae have culinary value, most of them are medicinals. Both their daisy-like flowers and their often strong-odored, bitter foliage have been widely used in the preparation of medicines since ancient times.

Herbs in the Labiate family are treasured by both cooks and chemists. This is because their leaves are very aromatic. As a result, the Labiate are used to flavor food and beverages, to keep stored linens fresh, and to perfume cosmetics. In addition, the foliage and essential oils are compounded into remedies for colds, minor stomach ailments, and insomnia.

Man utilizes every part of some herbs. For example, the root of caraway is served as a vegetable, its feathery leaves are

10

made into soups and salads, and its seeds are used for seasoning a wide variety of food ranging from sauerkraut to pastry and also are employed to scent perfume and soap. Incidentally, there is no proof that washing with soap scented with caraway oil improves the complexion but the ancient Greeks would approve of its use as a beauty aid. They maintained that caraway oil brought a rosy glow to the cheeks of pale-faced women.

Man and herbs

No one knows when herbs were first collected in the wild or planted in gardens, but it must have been at a very early date. A papyrus written in 1500 B.C. reveals that Egyptian doctors regularly prescribed herbal medicines for their patients. Because it is unlikely that unproven remedies would be mentioned in a papyrus, it is logical to assume that medicinal herbs—along with garlic, onions, sorrel, parsley, anise, coriander, and other culinary herbs—were commonplace in the Middle East long before scribes recorded the accomplishments of Egyptian physicians.

Anise

Fennel—the symbol of heroism

Used as food, seasoning, and incense in Biblical times, herbs are frequently mentioned in both the Old and New Testaments. Homer, Virgil, and other classical poets not only sang the praises of herbs but also employed their scents and the colors of their blossoms as adjectives. For example, Aristophanes describes "a saffron-colored gown" in *Lysistrata*. Saffron has been prized all through history for cooking, scenting perfume, and as the source of a gorgeous golden-yellow dye.

While poets engaged in flights of fancy, Hippocrates, the Greek physician who is regarded as the father of medicine, was practical. He used nearly five hundred different herbs to treat his patients. But Hippocrates' knowledge of herbs was scant compared to that of Pliny the Elder, most famous of Roman naturalists. Pliny zealously gathered information about herbs from every part of the then known world.

Not only educated men appreciated herbs. Ignorant peasants as well as scholars used them for condiments and food. Herbs were also employed to attract bees (whose honey acquired the characteristic odors of the plants) and were fed to sheep in order to impart a delicate flavor to their flesh. City dwellers also

12

used herbs for special purposes. For example, the citizens of Rome scattered horehound, a strong-smelling bitter herb, around their houses to drive away snakes and scorpions.

Caesar's legions carried herbs with them when they established settlements in Britain. But most of the species they introduced into England vanished when Rome abandoned that country. However, a few continued to be cultivated, and the native Saxons still collected wild species.

Through the years, traders and travelers transported herbs native to the Mediterranean region eastward to the Orient and brought herbs from Asia to Europe. While many of the seedlings carried to central Europe failed to survive the cold of winter, a number of them—along with native species—prospered in the

Early engraving shows an eastern trader bringing herbs to the coast for shipment to Europe.

gardens surrounding the great palace of Charlemagne at Aix-la-Chapelle in France. The ruler of the Holy Roman Empire was greatly interested in herbs. But his frequent decrees ordering his gardeners to grow certain varieties in the royal gardens were not prompted solely by a desire to experiment with the cultivation of new species. Charlemagne levied no direct taxes on his subjects so he depended on the sale of herbs raised at Aix-la-Chapelle to bring considerable revenue to his coffers.

While Charlemagne's herb garden was outstanding, it could not compare with those of certain European monasteries where herbs were grown to provide food for the monks and medicines for the sick. Perhaps the most famous of all these gardens was that of the hospice of St. Gall in Switzerland. Plans of St. Gall—the oldest known architectural plans—depict two plantings of herbs. One, near the institution's hospital, consisted of beds of "Physick" species. The other, located beside the kitchen, contained beds of herbs used in cooking.

Monastery herbalists not only concocted many of the remedies prescribed by medieval doctors but also devised new ones. Of course the monks did not approve of such customs as hanging a bunch of dill in doorways to prevent witches from entering houses, but they borrowed from pagan rites and used herbs in religious ceremonies.

As the use of herbs increased, so did the size of the monasteries' herb gardens. Actually, the cultivation of herbs by religious orders saved many introduced species from vanishing. Because of the numerous wars and devastating plagues that swept across Europe during the Middle Ages, most of the herb gardens owned by individuals either died out from neglect or were destroyed. But the plantings of the monks continued to thrive.

It was well they did. Herbs provided the only medicinal materials in medieval times. Apothecaries—the pharmacists of the Middle Ages—compounded herbs into medicines that supposedly cured every ill from sore eyes to cancer. Many of these remedies were inexpensive "simples." Others were high-priced, complicated mixtures.

The most costly of all herb blends were those based on the Mithridates Antidote. This famous draught was originally mixed by Mithridates, a tyrant ruler of Asia Minor who had murdered the rightful heirs to his throne. Because Mithridates feared that he, too, would be killed, he made an infusion of all the poisons that might possibly be placed in his food. He drank a small amount of this solution every day to build up an immunity to all poisons.

But Mithridates' brew did not save his life after all—he was stabbed to death. The directions for making his antidote were found on his body and the original formula and variations of it were highly esteemed as "cures" in medieval times. Certain of these potions contained the oils and leaves of one hundred different herbs. Traditionally, one of them was always rue. Actually, Mithridates was wise to include rue in his antidote. While this herb has medicinal value when taken in small amounts, it is a deadly poison in large doses.

Rue—herb of grace and symbol of regret

As the centuries passed, the use of both culinary and medicinal herbs greatly increased throughout Europe, except in England. Therefore, after conquering Britain in 1066, the Normans sent to France for a wide variety of herbs. While certain of these plants used by their new rulers to season food did not appeal to the English, those that were curative agents became welcome additions to the native medicinal herbs listed in Anglo-Saxon leechbooks.

Other herbs were brought to England by knights returning from the Crusades and were planted in the gardens of the great manor houses. Each estate had an herb woman—often the mistress of the manor—who was responsible for the raising, drying, and storing of herbs for future use. Because of the lack of trained doctors, these women also assumed the task of treating the sick and wounded with medicines made from herbs.

Meanwhile, both men and women herbalists wandered from village to village peddling tinctures, ointments, and "balms." Certain of these individuals were experts on the use of medicinal herbs. Others were charlatans. The latter were derided by Chaucer (1342–1400) in *The Canterbury Tales*, a series of poems that vividly depict the peoples and customs of medieval England. Incidentally, Chaucer had a considerable knowledge of herbs and—like Bacon, Herrick, Shakespeare, and many other

Summer savory

Borage, when crushed in wine, supposedly gave courage to all who drank it in ancient Rome. Today, the herb is used by cooks because of its cucumberlike juice.

English authors, dramatists, and poets—filled his writings with herb lore.

Despite roving herbalists and the herb women of the manors, the monasteries continued to supply large numbers of people with medicinal herbs. When Henry the Eighth ordered the monasteries to close their doors in 1543, he made sure that the sick and ailing did not suffer because of a lack of herbs. He decreed that the curates of local churches should assume the responsibility of providing them. Eventually, however, it was the wives and daughters of the curates who tended the parish herb garden, prepared medicines, and administered them. By the early eighteenth century, practically every countrywoman was raising culinary and medicinal herbs and collecting wild species for use in her household. Thus it was natural for the descendants of these cottage gardeners to carry herb seeds and cuttings with them when they left England to settle in the New World.

The first herb garden was established in America before the Pilgrims landed at Plymouth in 1620. But some of the species which Captain John Mason had planted in Newfoundland in 1619 winter-killed. Others prospered. So did many of the herbs set out by the various colonists. For example, chicory—which had been brought to Europe from Asia—became a common weed shortly after being sown by Governor John Winthrop in Boston to feed his sheep. As a result, by 1672, John Josselyn could compile a relatively long list "of such herbe among us which doth thrive . . . ."

Catnip has long been brewed as a tea to cure insomnia. It is still used in many medicines but probably is appreciated most of all by cats and other members of the feline family.

Besides using herbs that they had known in England, the settlers acquired knowledge about native herbs from the Indians, who not only employed the plants in religious ceremonies but also utilized them as food and medicines. In return, the colonists taught the Indians how to make herbal teas and other medicines with the species introduced from England.

As homesteaders trekked westward, they carried carefully wrapped bunches of herb seedlings and herb seeds harvested from the gardens they were abandoning. On reaching their destinations, pioneer women grubbed a plot for an herb garden while their menfolk broke the prairie with their plows. The plants they raised not only provided "greens" and added zest to the simple fare of the frontiersmen but also furnished medicines that proved invaluable to families living far from a doctor.

Because birds and wind scattered the seeds of the culinary and medicinal herbs planted by pioneer women, patches of certain herbs became commonplace throughout the countryside. Among them was wormwood. Used for generations to repel insects, particularly moths, and as a wormifuge, wormwood is extremely acrid. This is why the herb is used in the Bible as a symbol of the bitterness felt by mankind.

As small settlements grew into thriving cities, herbs ceased to be an important food, while the prescriptions of physicians took the place of household remedies compounded from herbs. However, many species of herbs continued to be employed by reputable manufacturers of medicines, and herbs still were used by itinerant quacks who sold herbal elixirs "guaranteed" to rejuvenate the old, grow hair, and cure every ill known to man.

Today, herbs are valued more as condiments than as medicinals. While a great number of herbs are listed in the *United States Pharmacopeia,* a book which describes officially recognized drugs, chemicals, and medicines, the majority of species once used by doctors have been replaced by artificial com-

A selection of herbs for a green salad—

chicory (french endive)

endive

Iceberg lettuce

loose leaf lettuce

The young leaves of dandelion make a delicious early spring salad when wilted with hot vinegar and bacon. Dandelion is also made into wine.

Once a rare and highly prized herb, mustard is now a common condiment. Here mustard seed is being harvested by machinery.

pounds. Similarly, synthetic dyes, flavorings, and scents have greatly reduced the importance of herbs to industry.

The chances are that the herbalists of yesteryear who tramped the fields seeking herbs and the devout brothers who cultivated the gardens at St. Gall would be amazed to learn that man can duplicate the oils, scents, and flavors of herbs. But they would be delighted at the ever increasing interest in culinary herbs. Imagine their astonishment if they could see the large displays of herbs from all over the world in supermarkets or if they could visit one of the many shops in large cities that sell nothing but herbs and spices.

The old and the new—the implements in this picture are similar to those used by herbalists of yesteryear but the boxes of herb leaves and seed were packed by modern machinery.

2
Raising Herbs

Sage

"How does your garden grow?"

Few plantings are more attractive than formal herb gardens. Not only are the herbs arranged so that they form an intricate pattern but also the plants are placed so that their varying heights, differing growth habits, contrasting foliage, and diversified blossoms blend together to form "a design within a design." Artistic herb plantings of this type—called knot gardens—were the pride of the owners of large estates in Elizabethan England. Today, many of the herb gardens designed during that period are copied or modified in botanical parks, in nurseries, and by individuals who raise herbs as a hobby.

No simple task is the planning, laying out, and maintenance of a formal herb garden. It requires expert knowledge of both herbs and landscaping. But amateur gardeners can create charming effects by setting a variety of carefully chosen herbs in a circular, oval, or triangular plot.

However, herbs do not demand even a semi-formal setting. They can be raised in rock gardens, in vegetable plots, along foundations, outside the kitchen door—the location most favored by the family cook—and beside pathways, as well as on windowsills or under artificial light. Novices will do well to limit the space and the number of their herbs until they have acquired

22

Diagram of the design within a design of a knot garden— 1 Thyme, 2 Sweet violet, 3 Lavender, 4 Germander or rosemary

A formal herb garden—an Elizabethan knot garden—grows in Brooklyn.

firsthand knowledge of the characteristics of different species and learned which varieties are most suitable for their purposes.

Cultivation of herbs

Some herbs thrive in both cool and warm regions. Other species require special climatic conditions. But, generally speaking, the majority of herbs are easily grown. While most species demand considerable sunshine, a number of herbs, including balm, the mints, parsley, and tarragon, do well in partial shade.

Tarragon, which will grow in partial shade, is used to flavor vinegar.

Data detailing a particular herb's preference for light or shade, along with identification as to whether it is an annual, biannual, or perennial, usually appear on seed packets. Information about the herbs that flourish in a specific area can be found in garden encyclopedias available in public libraries.

Light, well-drained soil is best for most herbs but the majority will prosper when planted in heavy, well-drained loam if sand

24

is added. Conversely, if the soil contains a large amount of sand, peat moss or other humus should be worked into it. All soil is best tested for acidity, and agricultural lime should be applied if needed.

Although bonemeal or superphosphate will encourage sturdy growth, use them sparingly. Actually, a great many herbs develop best in poor soils. If planted in rich soil they develop lush foliage but the leaves contain only small amounts of the oils that give the various species their characteristic scents and taste. Moreover, too much fertilizer promotes soft growth in perennials and increases the chances of their being winter-killed.

In general, herbs dislike "wet feet." However, the mints, angelica, bergamot, and parsley thrive in moist soil. All these herbs, particularly the mints, appreciate frequent waterings. Most other species need watering only occasionally except in extremely dry periods.

Parsley thrives in moist soil and under ideal growing conditions produces foliage like this.

Any gardener who has impatiently waited for a prized rose-bush to bloom, only to have its freshly opened flowers ravaged by Japanese beetles, has good reason to envy herbalists. By and large, herbs are not subject to invasions by pests nor do they suffer from disease if properly grown. However, rust may appear on the leaves of certain species. When this happens, the plants should be sprayed with sulphur and the old stems burned. Dry weather may spur mites to attack sage but these are easily repelled with a soapsuds spray.

Although herbs are resistant to pests, this basil plant is being eaten by cutworms.

While a few herbs resent transplanting, and must be sown during the late autumn or early spring in the place where they are to stand, most species can be started indoors. If flats—the shallow, coverless boxes used by professional growers—are not available, seeds can be planted in pots, cut-down milk cartons, and the plastic packages in which cottage cheese and other dairy products are sold. Holes should be punched in the bottoms of cartons and plastic containers and covered with a layer of crock—gravel or bits of broken clay pots—to insure proper drainage. Crock should also be placed in the bottoms of pots as it keeps any surplus moisture beneath the soil.

26

Although many gardeners prefer to start herb seeds in shredded sphagnum moss or vermiculite, a mixture composed of one-third sand, one-third compost (peat moss), and one-third soil is most satisfactory. Before the soil is mixed with the other ingredients, it should be sterilized either by baking or by being drenched with boiling water.

After sowing, keep the growing medium damp but not wet. Containers can be watered in two ways. They can be sprinkled with a fine mist—bottles with plungers that formerly held window-cleaning solutions make excellent sprinklers—or placed in water until they soak up sufficient moisture. If the containers are covered with a sheet of glass or with plastic held down with an elastic band, they will not have to be watered frequently. If watering is necessary or if excess condensation occurs, these coverings are easily removed.

During germination, an herb planting should be placed where the temperature does not rise above seventy degrees during the day or drop below fifty degrees at night. While basil will sprout within seven days, most herbs take three or four weeks to "come up." When the seedlings appear, the glass or plastic coverings are removed and the containers located so that the young plants receive as much sunshine as possible. Turn the containers around every other day so that the seedlings will not lean toward the light.

Because a stream of water is apt to bruise small seedlings or wash away soil, young plants should never be watered from above. Instead, their containers should be placed in room-temperature water and left until the soil becomes damp. Avoid overwatering to prevent damping off—the withering of tender shoots.

Once seedlings have developed two pairs of leaves, they can be lifted out of their container—an old fork is an excellent tool for this purpose—with as much soil as possible clinging to the roots and transplanted outdoors. Water well and cover with an inverted pot or other "parasol" to shield them from the sun until they are established.

Protection for young plants—"parasols" made of paper bag, plastic dome, plastic container, cardboard box.

During the growing season, herbs should be weeded and cultivated like all garden vegetation by breaking up the soil around the plants with a hoe. Both watering and fertilizing should be regulated carefully. Too much water will cause the plants to rot while overfeeding will make them straggly.

Perennial herbs such as chives, parsley, and tansy that die down to the ground in the fall require special attention in late

Since its introduction into the New World, horehound has spread rapidly and become a noxious weed. Cattle will not eat it, but the plant's juice is used in cough syrups and lozenges.

autumn. Their dead tops should be removed before they become covered with snow. On the other hand, the dead growth of horehound, lavender, rosemary, rue, sage, and other shrublike herbs should not be cut off until the following spring. It is also good practice to provide perennial species with protection where winters are severe. Hay, straw, branches of discarded Christmas trees, bushel baskets, and leaves can be used.

There are two methods of saving perennials that are not hardy in a particular region. They can either be wintered in a cold frame or potted and kept on a sunny windowsill until spring.

Herbs indoors

One does not have to live in the country or suburbs to enjoy the beauty of herbs and to use their freshly picked leaves in cooking. Basil, balm, chives, dill, fennel, lemon verbena, parsley, rosemary, sage, summer savory, sweet marjoram, tarragon, and several of the mints thrive in windowboxes, pots, or wooden tubs. While certain of these species develop into large plants outdoors, they become dwarfed when grown in small containers. However, when raised in wooden tubs—ideal for rooftop gardens because they do not blow over in high winds—they reach their maximum growth.

Although brightly painted or stained wooden tubs add much to the appeal of an herb garden on a roof, terrace, or balcony,

This pepper, grown indoors in a big pail, can be put out on the terrace on sunny days.

the natural weathering of redwood tubs is even more attractive. Incidentally, redwood tubs, having been treated with a preservative, do not need to be stained or painted to protect them from the weather.

A windowbox of herbs set on an inside sill not only makes any room more attractive but also fills the air with delightful fragrance. While it is necessary to bruise a leaf or two of some herbs gently to release their pungent scents, one has only to enter a room in which mint is growing to catch its tangy odor. However, while a windowbox herb garden is a source of delight to both plant lovers and cooks, windowboxes are difficult to move from one location to another. On the other hand, pots can be transported from room to room for varying decorative effects.

Generally speaking, herbs grow best in pots six to eight inches in diameter. Clay pots blend best with herb foliage but must be handled carefully to avoid breakage. They also have to be

Sweet marjoram, sacred to Venus, goddess of love

Herbs that take well to being grown in pots—hyssop, European mint used as remedy for bruises; burnet; lovage, a celery-like herb (from left)

watered more frequently than plastic pots. But the latter—which are not likely to shatter when hit or dropped—do not "breathe" and, as a result, hold moisture. Therefore, if they are watered too frequently the soil becomes soggy and the plants in them either grow poorly or rot.

In addition to regular waterings and a once a month feeding with a soluble-in-water houseplant food, it is good practice to give potted herbs a thorough soaking every week. The easiest way to do this is to place the pots in water and let them stand for an hour. Incidentally, placing the pots in a deep tray filled with gravel and water will not only assure proper drainage and sufficient humidity but also prevent water stains on windowsills and tables. Be sure and put enough gravel into the tray so that the water does not come in contact with the pots.

Because most herbs demand full sunshine, set indoor plantings in the sunniest window. If no window receives sun for several hours a day, an indoor herb garden should be limited to such shade-loving species as basil, oregano, parsley, or sweet mar-

31

*One of the most pop-
ular culinary herbs,
oregano must be used
with care because of
its pungency.*

joram. But there is no limit to the number of herbs that can be
grown under fluorescent fixtures equipped with "daylight" bulbs.
Sold under various trade names, these fixtures, designed for indoor gardening, are manufactured in a wide variety of sizes.

Plants for indoor herb gardens can either be raised from seed
or purchased. While some garden supply centers offer single
plants, others only sell herbs in flats containing six or more
plants. When removing plants from a flat, care must be taken
to avoid too much damage to their intertwined roots. The best
method is to slice the dirt surrounding each plant down to the
bottom of the flat with a sharp knife, water the flat from below,
let it stand overnight, and gently scoop out the plants the next

*A flat of herbs. Many herbs can be propagated by cuttings. To make a
cutting, shear off a stem and keep it in damp sand until roots form.*

A crowded flat of parsley before transplanting

day. They should lift easily and have a cube of soil clinging to their roots.

Container-raised herbs require the same attention as other house plants—sufficient light and warmth, humidity, infrequent but regular feedings, and proper watering. Pot-grown herbs will be more attractive if they are shaped by trimming—a task that can be accomplished without effort if care is taken when the leaves are cut for culinary purposes.

HARVESTING HERBS

The tender, fresh, aromatic leaves of all annual herbs can be picked just as soon as they have made sufficient growth. However, no species can withstand the shock of being trimmed constantly. Therefore, gardeners who desire a large and continual supply of a particular annual herb should either plant a long row of it or make successive sowings of seed so that old plants can be replaced.

Foliage can also be cut from the majority of perennial herbs the first season. But it is best to make only a scant harvest. After the plants are established they may be cut three or four times each season. No leaves should be taken from certain perennial herbs the first year—these species are identified on the seed packets. If perennial seedlings are purchased, it is wise to

Ancient herbalists relied on the weather, charms, and their experience to dry herbs. Today, manufacturers use complicated machinery.

ask if any foliage can be taken until the plants have over-wintered.

Fresh leaves can be gathered from an indoor herb garden throughout the year. But the only way foliage from outdoor plantings can be utilized after the growing season is to dry it. There are two ways of drying herbs. One is to tie small bunches of sprigs together, hang them in a sheltered, airy spot to dry, then bottle in a tightly sealed container. The other method is to strip the leaves by hand and scatter them over a tray or screen placed in a shady spot where air circulates freely. It usually takes about two weeks for the leaves to become completely dry. All dried herb foliage should be kept in a dark place or in opaque bottles as light affects its flavor.

The best time to cut herbs for future use is when they are coming into bloom. This is when the leaves are saturated with

To dry, herb foliage can be hung in bunches in an airy spot (parsley), or spread out on a tray or screen (caraway).

the essential oils that give each species its distinctive aroma. Sprigs should be gathered early in the morning after the sun has dried the dew but before it has warmed the foliage. Use a sharp scissors to avoid mangling the stems and take care not to shear the top growth of perennial plants or they may winter-kill. All foliage may be cut off annual species before the frost nips it.

Although most herbs can be dried successfully, certain species lose much of their flavor after being picked. However, this can be partially prevented by special techniques. Directions for drying some of the most commonly grown herbs in this group are given in the next chapter.

Herbs such as dill which are valued for both foliage and seed should not be picked until their flower-like seed heads have matured. Then they should be cut so that the seed heads fall into a paper bag which is kept open until the seeds dry. Before bottling them, winnow the chaff by spreading the seeds on a sheet of newspaper and blowing gently.

Both herb leaves and blossoms can be frozen by the same procedure used to freeze vegetables, fruits, and berries. Mixtures of various herbs can also be frozen. *No herbs should be refrozen once defrosted.*

Dill heads should be cut so they fall into a paper bag which is kept open until the herb dries. Dill was thought to relieve hiccoughs and keep witches away, and is known to combine with cucumbers to produce excellent pickles.

3
Herbs: Fact and Fiction

Rosemary

". . . ask not for a larger garden."

Folklore holds that some herbs will thrive only if planted in a particular location or beside certain other herbs. Ancient custom also decrees that herbs must be harvested at specific times. For example, it was once a common superstition throughout Europe that herbs gathered on Midsummer's Eve (June 23), when supernatural beings supposedly roamed the Earth, were particularly aromatic. Similar beliefs concerning the picking of herbs are found in Asia and among the inhabitants of the New World.

Until comparatively recent times, many peoples were convinced that it was necessary to chant sacred incantations when harvesting herbs. It was also believed that herbs not only lost their value as medicinals but also their magic-working properties if cut with an iron tool. This is why the Druids used a sickle made of gold to cut the herb sprigs they employed in their secret rites.

Actually, there are more legends, traditions, superstitions, and rituals connected with herbs than with any other plants. While few if any modern herbalists maintain that mugwort placed under a saddle will make a horse "travaile fresh and lustily," hold that vervain worn as an amulet protects one from evil, or

36

are convinced of the truth of any of the other age-old beliefs about herbs, a knowledge of such lore adds greatly to the enjoyment of raising herbs.

Obviously, no book the size of this one could list all the herb lore that has accumulated over the centuries. As a result, space can be found to record only the lore associated with those herbs most commonly grown in gardens and pots by novices. Along with these fascinating fictions, definite instructions for raising and using these species are given.

Balm

Melissa officinalis is a native of the fields of southern Europe. It grows best in partial shade and prefers a rather sandy soil. Because the seeds of balm—frequently called lemon balm—are extremely small, they should be mixed with sand before planting to insure an evenly distributed sowing.

As indicated, when seedlings develop their second pair of leaves they can be transplanted—either into the garden or singly into containers. The later should be at least eight inches in diameter as balm has a tendency to spread and lie close to the ground. Indoors or out, thick lush growth is encouraged by pinching back the first top leaves after a plant has recovered from the shock of transplanting.

Gardeners, like fishermen, must have patience. Do not pick any foliage the first year, no matter how well a plant grows, until the pale yellow flowers appear. Then, and then only, a *few* short sprigs may be cut. After the first year, several bountiful harvests can be gathered annually—balm should be sheared back two or three times every season.

Because balm is very aromatic and has a pleasing scent and taste, it has long been used by manufacturers of perfumes and liqueurs. In the home, balm is employed to flavor lemonade and other summer drinks. It is also an ideal seasoning for a wide range of foods, particularly soups and salads.

No one knows for sure whether or not the balm referred to in the Bible, mentioned frequently by historians, and praised by countless poets is the herb or the balm of Gilead (*Balsamodendron opobalsam*), a tree native to India. But there is no doubt that the herb was used for centuries as a medicinal. Ancient Arab physicians prescribed it for hypochondria and heart trouble. Greek doctors pulverized the foliage and made it into poultices to apply to the bites of snakes, and also of rabid dogs, although it was ineffective. They also recommended balm sprigs steeped in wine to reduce fevers. Because balm induces perspiration, the sprigs lowered the patient's temperature. But the peoples of yesteryear would be shocked to learn that balm is among the herbs no longer considered to have medicinal value. Their faith in these plants was so great that any attempt to convince them that the herbs had no curative powers would have been a waste of time.

Like the Greeks, the Romans regarded balm as a potent medicine and invested it with magic powers. They even rubbed the strong-scented leaves over furniture to drive evil spirits out of their homes. The Romans set the highest value on balm as a bee-alluring plant and relished honey made from its flowers. This is why Virgil, as skilled a beekeeper as he was a poet, planted balm near his hives.

Credited with great curative powers in ancient Greece and Rome and praised by poets throughout history, balm is a popular pot herb today.

Medieval apothecaries throughout Europe mixed dried balm leaves—which they bought from traders—in both "simples" and complicated cures. This widespread use of the herb led to its becoming a common plant in kitchen gardens and, by the mid-seventeenth century, it was noted that "Balm groweth in almost every Country Housewife's garden . . . it driveth away poisons arising from melancholly." Another English writer credited balm with even greater attributes. He claimed that it was a remedy "for all the ills that flesh is heir to."

Rural Frenchmen, like English countrymen, considered balm a sure cure for many ailments. As a result, they firmly believed that the Wandering Jew, whom legend held was doomed to roam the Earth until Judgment Day, saved the life of a dying farmer with a tincture of balm and beer. Educated Frenchmen were more credulous. However, they maintained that balm, crushed with other herbs and mixed with wine, relieved headaches. This is why the last three kings of France granted royal patents to the Carmelite Friars to manufacture a lotion they called *Eau de Mellise des Cannes* (Water of the Balm from Cannes).

BASIL

There are several varieties of basil. The original sweet basil (*Ocimum basilicum*) originated in the Near East and was introduced into Europe from Greece and Rome. In addition to this species, modern seedsmen offer dwarf basil (*Ocimum minimum*), curly basil (*Ocimum crispum*), and the rather tender lemon basil (*Ocimum citriodora*).

The various types of basil differ greatly in size and in the color of their stems and crumpled, heart-shaped leaves. All are annuals and make charming houseplants. The most satisfactory species for either garden or pots are the green or purple-leaved strains of dwarf basil and of curly basil.

Seed sown in well-drained soil and placed in full sun sprouts in about a week, and the seedlings rapidly develop into mature

Few herbs have as many traditions, superstitions, and legends associated with them as basil.

plants bearing spikes of small, tubular white flowers on the tops of their branches. Leaves can be harvested just as soon as they are big enough to pick. The herb's foliage gives a delightful clovelike flavor to eggs, meats, poultry, and vegetables. A basil leaf on a slice of freshly picked tomato is a culinary delight. However, it is well to remember the warning of an early herbalist when using basil for seasoning—"Basil imparts a grateful flavour if not too strong."

Basil can be dried, but drying is not worth the effort because the leaves lose much of their aroma and flavor in the process. But

One of the first herbs cultivated by the colonists in America, basil is grown under irrigation in a field in California.

if one wishes to attempt to dry basil, the foliage should be gathered when a plant begins to bloom.

Basil is employed commercially to season vinegars, certain salad dressings, and canned tomato paste. While basil is not a basic ingredient in all brands of factory-produced tomato sauce, the herb is always included in the various recipes of home-made tomato sauce that have been handed down from mother to daughter for centuries in Mediterranean countries.

Man has long displayed mixed feelings about basil. Folklore maintains that it is both a sacred herb and one of the Devil's favorite plants. While modern Italians regard a sprig of basil as a love token, the herb was considered a symbol of hatred in classical Greece where the doctors also disagreed as to its medicinal value. Although Hippocrates prescribed basil, Galen —the first physician to recognize the importance of a patient's pulse rate—held it unfit for human consumption. Meanwhile, Arab doctors esteemed the plant highly. So did Pliny, Rome's leading herbalist. However, Pliny was convinced that basil would not thrive unless it was abused and insisted that "it must be sown with curses and ugly words."

Incidentally, because scorpions were often discovered under basil in Rome, Pliny maintained that the herb's leaves propagated scorpions. This led to the unfounded belief that basil foliage was a specific cure for scorpion stings.

Like the Greeks, early English herbalists had conflicting views about basil. Some were sure it was a lethal herb—a conviction based on the tradition that basil would not grow if planted near rue, the herb traditionally used as an antidote for poison. Other writers maintained that smelling basil leaves was beneficial to the head and also claimed they produced " a cheerful and merry heart."

Basil may have stimulated cheerfulness in England but it was linked with sorrow in both Egypt and Persia, where it was grown on graves. The herb is still associated with death in India—

41

where it is also thought to be a sure cure for snakebite and many ills—and considered one of the most holy of plants. The Hindu custom of growing pots of basil in memory of deceased loved ones is the source of both Boccaccio's story in the *Decameron* and John Keats' poem "Isabella or the Pot of Basil." These tragic tales recount the sufferings of a beautiful young woman who buried the head of her murdered lover in a pot of basil and watered it daily with her tears.

CHIVES

Most members of the lily family have subtle scents, but those classified as herbs—garlic, leeks, onions, scallions, and shallots—have strong odors. Chives (*Allium schoanoprasum*) is not as pungent an herb as its close relatives. As a result, chives are as widely used as a piquant seasoning today as they were in their native China more than five thousand years ago.

Chives, sometimes called rush onions, are a hardy perennial and grow in clumps. The foliage is thin, deep-green, and cylindrical, like straws. Given plenty of sunshine and set in rich, rocky soil, chives will prosper in temperate and warm climates outdoors. Because neither the leaves nor the flower stalks, which bear small pompom-like lavender blossoms, rise more than six to eight inches, chives are an ideal plant for the indoor herb garden.

Chives can be raised from seed sown in rich, pebbly soil. But the seed germinates very slowly so it is more satisfactory to purchase a clump of chives composed of a number of tiny, foliage-bearing bulbs. Few mature herbs are more easily acquired— chive clumps are sold in most supermarkets.

If kept free of weeds and cultivated regularly, chives multiply so rapidly in the garden that they must be dug up every two or three years and the clump divided. An indoor planting will also soon overcrowd a large pot. When this occurs, the clump should be subdivided and repotted.

42

Chives thrive outdoors in rocky soil but are easy to raise in containers if placed in full sun. Right: *Close-up of chive blossoms.*

Chives can be harvested at any time. While the thin foliage can be snapped off easily with the fingers, cutting it carefully with scissors keeps a plant attractively trimmed. Moreover, a sharp tool should be used to slice the flower stalks close to the ground after they bloom. The bulbs—which can be pickled or used in recipes calling for small onions—are removed by simply grasping a leaf close to its roots and pulling gently.

One does not have to be a gourmet chef to employ chives in cooking. Chives give zest to a long menu of dishes ranging from appetizers to scrambled eggs. But blending with cream cheese is the most popular use of chives. Spread on freshly baked rye bread, the piquant flavor of "chive-cheese" is an inexpensive but truly epicurean treat.

Garlic, leeks, and onions are featured in legends and have long been credited with magical powers. But herb lore has neglected chives. One of the few herbs never connected with either the forces of good or evil, neither have chives been considered a sovereign remedy for illness. However, the ancient herbalists included chives among the most useful plants they claimed were revealed to man by the gods when the world was young.

43

MINT

All the mints of the genus *Mentha* are hardy perennials that grow one to two feet tall. The most commonly raised species in outdoor gardens are spearmint (*Mentha spicata*) and peppermint (*Mentha piperita*). American apple mint (*Mentha gentilis variegata*) and orange mint (*Mentha citrata*) are also popular with herbalists. Besides thriving outdoors, these four varieties also flourish in containers.

Even if these four mints had no culinary value, their beauty would justify their inclusion in any collection of herbs. Both peppermint and spearmint have lance-shaped, toothed leaves— the deep-green, purple-tinged foliage of peppermint is broad; that of spearmint is yellower in tone and tapers more acutely at the tips. Both plants have slender, purple-red flowers. The broad leaves of orange mint are also touched with purple and its short spikes of purple blossoms give off a delightful orange scent.

Spearmint

Curlemint

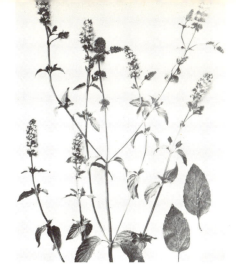

Peppermint

Apple mint with its almost square stems, smooth gray-green, yellow-streaked leaves, and delicate purple flowers is not only a handsome plant but its foliage has the odor and taste of fresh fruit.

Mints can be grown from seed but are best propagated by divisions or runners (stems with good roots) placed in moist, rich soil in a shady spot. The mints require frequent cultivation —soil in containers can be "hoed" with a fork or nail—and resent weeds.

The Latin name of pennyroyal, Mentha pulegium, *reveals that the plant is one of the mints and that its greatest use throughout history has been to drive away* pulices—*body lice and fleas.*

If unchecked, the mints will crowd out other plants, and they quickly fill the largest pots. Overcrowded containers can be thinned by pulling some of the runners, while the spread of outdoor plantings is easily halted by surrounding mint roots with the aluminum stripping available in garden-supply centers.

Not only can a reasonable number of sprigs and leaves be picked off a mature mint plant at any time but also mint will grow better if it is subjected to severe pruning occasionally. However, if a large number of sprigs and flowering tips are cut after a plant has gone to seed, the plant is likely to die.

Oils extracted from peppermint and spearmint are used in the manufacture of confections, chewing gum, mouth washes, liqueurs, perfumes, and soaps. In the kitchen, whole or crushed mint is employed to flavor iced tea and other beverages. Mint also imparts an exotic taste to practically every dish from soup to ice cream.

Legend holds that when Pluto, lord of the underworld, fell in love with the beautiful nymph Menthe, Proserpine, whom he had abducted and married, became insane with jealousy. In her rage, she transformed Menthe into a low-growing plant so that all who walked through the woods would trample her. But Proserpine's desire for revenge was not satisfied—she unthinkingly gave the plant a delightful scent and, as a result, whenever mint is crushed, its fragrance recalls the beauty of the nymph for whom it is named.

Both the Greeks and the Romans used mint as a strewing herb—as did the residents of Elizabethan England—and also rubbed its foliage on tabletops before meals. Homer, Hippocrates, Ovid, and Pliny made frequent reference to the value of mint as a medicinal and flavoring agent. "The smell of mint," wrote Pliny, "doth stir up on the mind and taste a greedy desire for meat." The Greeks and Romans also considered mint a valuable medicinal. So did medieval doctors—they treated ills ranging from earache to ulcers with it.

Because there was no differentiation between the various mints until late in the Middle Ages, no one knows which species made up the "tithes of mint" referred to in the New Testament. It may have been peppermint, which probably originated in Hindustan and was brought to the Near East at a very early date.

Long before mint was included among the "precious herbs" brought to the New World, the American Indians were using various mints to mask human scent on their traps. The Mesk-waki of Wisconsin relieved headaches with snuff manufactured from the leaves of different mints and also blew this mixture into the nostrils of the dying in hopes of reviving them. Mesk-waki braves were convinced that any snake could be captured easily if a cud of mint was spit onto a stick and held in front of its nose.

PARSLEY

Petroselinum hortense is thought to be a native of Sardinia. A biennial—or, if not allowed to go to seed, a perennial— parsley has divided foliage and bears tiny gold flowers in flat terminal clusters. Like most biennials, a rosette of leaves appears the first year, the flower stalks being produced the second season. To prevent a plant from going to seed, the blossoms should be cut off as soon as they appear.

The various varieties of parsley are distinguished by their leaves. Most popular are the double-curved and moss-leaved types whose foliage not only makes an attractive garnish for many foods but also a pretty as well as practical border for an herb garden. Fern-leaved parsley—often called Italian parsley —has much coarser foliage than its kin and has a definite pungent taste.

The least known of all types of parsley is the turnip-rooted

47

Small pot of curly parsley

Turnip-rooted parsley

species, which, despite its name, has a root resembling that of a miniature parsnip. When cooked, the root tastes like celery. Besides being eaten as a vegetable, turnip-rooted parsley is used in pharmaceutical preparations.

Parsley requires rich, damp soil. The seeds germinate very slowly but soaking them in lukewarm water for twenty-four hours before planting will speed up the process. When sowing parsley indoors, merely press the seeds into the soil. Seeds planted outdoors should be scattered on the surface and then pushed into the ground by covering them with a flat board and walking on it. Because parsley takes so long to come up (about two weeks), English herbalists claimed that the seed visited the Devil three times before it sprouted.

48

Thin seedlings to at least six inches apart in the garden, and place only one plant in a pot. The latter should be kept evenly moist with lukewarm water and placed on a cool windowsill in partial shade.

Fully formed foliage can be cut at any time. While parsley can be dried, it loses much of its flavor in the process. This can be partially overcome by stripping the leaves off the stems and dipping them in a quart of boiling water containing a teaspoonful of salt for two or three seconds. Shake the leaves to remove as much of the solution as possible, then spread the foliage to dry.

Manufacturers employ parsley in wine-making and to color cheese. Cooks not only use it as a garnish but also as a seasoning for creamed vegetables, omelets, fish, sauces, soups, and in melted butter for "new" potatoes.

Parsley was highly regarded as a medicinal in ancient times. Both Greek and Roman physicians prescribed it. The Greeks believed that parsley was particularly effective in the treatment of kidney stones. As a result, they called the plant *petroselinon* (rock breaker).

Along with employing parsley as a cure, the Romans and the Egyptians used the herb as a garnish and as a seasoning. Parsley garlands which were thought to absorb wine fumes and prevent drunkenness were worn by diners at Greek banquets. Moreover, at the end of these feasts, all present chewed parsley to sweeten their breaths which normally reeked with the odor of two other herbs—garlic and onion.

The Greeks also strewed parsley on floors during festive occasions, and crowned youths and maidens during religious celebrations with wreaths made from it, while country swains expressed their love by giving their sweethearts chaplets of the herb. Meanwhile, winners of events at the Nemean and Isthmian Games—two of the most important athletic contests in ancient Greece—were awarded garlands of wild parsley.

Besides weaving the plant into funeral decorations, the Greeks planted it on graves. Because parsley was sacred to the dead, Plutarch, the famous historian, claimed that an army of Greek soldiers about to charge an enemy retreated in panic because they saw a train of parsley-laden mules on the way to market.

Many classical writers mention parsley. The majority, like Homer, who described "soft meadows blossomed with violets and parsley," stress the herb's attractive foliage. In later centuries many English poets, including Gay, Herrick, Keats, and Shakespeare, also praised the herb. There was good reason. The English were convinced that parsley purified the blood, removed hair, improved the mind, and caused visions. They also believed that parsley seed sown on Good Friday grew double. On the other hand, Englishmen maintained that if an individual transplanted the herb, there would be a death in his family and Satan would take over his garden. British herb lore also holds that while a desire for parsley is an omen of death, no harm will come to those who steal it. Moreover, anyone who gives parsley away or accepts it as a gift will be unlucky.

To most people, parsley is merely a decorative addition to a meal. Actually, it is a very valuable food. High in vitamins A and C, parsley not only contains a considerable amount of iron but also is a source of calcium, niacin, and vitamins B-1 and B-2. Medieval monks would be delighted to learn that nutritional biochemists have discovered this data by analyzing parsley, but they would not be surprised at these results. They always tossed parsley into their fishponds whenever the fish appeared to be ailing.

ROSEMARY

This herb is a native of the rocky Mediterranean Coast where it thrives on cliffs overhanging the water, its gray-green foliage

Rosemary—the herb of remembrance

merging into the ocean mist. Because rosemary flourishes near salt water, botanists have named it *Rosmarinus officinalis*—dew of the sea.

A slow-growing perennial evergreen, under ideal conditions rosemary develops into a shrubby bush five-to-six feet tall. Indoors it rarely grows higher than fifteen inches. Curved like pine needles, deep green on the upper side and silvery gray beneath, the narrow leaves have a spicy, pungent fragrance. The flowers range in color from a delicate to a purplish blue. Usually, the blossoms do not appear until a plant is at least two years old.

Although rosemary is ordinarily propagated either by cuttings or division it can be raised from seed which germinates in three to four weeks. If seed is sown, it should be covered with a mere dusting of soil.

"The plant that loves the sea" prefers a light, sandy, limy soil. You can make sure it has all the lime it requires by sprinkling a pinch over the soil occasionally. But take care that the lime does not come in contact with the stalks or leaves.

Rosemary demands considerable sunshine, whether planted in the garden or in containers. Because rosemary grows vigorously, care should be taken to place outdoor plantings in positions where they will not shade sun-loving herbs. Moreover, individual plants should be spaced about two feet apart so that they will have sufficient room to spread. Indoors, rosemary requires a pot eight-to-ten inches in diameter. In both garden and house the herb needs frequent waterings and also should be trimmed regularly to keep it low and bushy. When planted in gardens in colder regions, it is best either to mulch rosemary heavily or to overwinter it on a windowsill.

One or two rosemary plants will provide the average family with more than enough fresh and dried leaves to flavor eggs, fish, meats, soups, and vegetables. The foliage should be used as soon as it is big enough to pick—young leaves have more pungency than old ones.

There are countless legends, traditions, and superstitions about rosemary. Not only has the herb been considered the emblem of friendship and the symbol of remembrance for hundreds of years, but also it has long been endowed with magical powers. If ancient beliefs are true, rosemary keeps witches away, provides protection from the evil eye, guards both the dead and the living from harm, brings good fortune, and, if placed in a bridal bouquet, insures a happy marriage. Welsh cooks claim that food stirred with a spoon fashioned from rosemary wood becomes more nutritious. A conserve made of rosemary blossoms eaten with bread and salt was thought by the early English herbalists to "comfort the heart." But students in ancient Greece probably made the most unusual use of the plant—they twined rosemary sprigs in their hair while studying to stimulate their brains.

In England, until comparatively recent times, it was the custom for maidens to place rosemary in one shoe and thyme in the other on St. Agnes Eve, the twentieth of January. After putting one shoe on each side of their beds, they went to sleep, confident that they would see the faces of their future husbands in their dreams.

Because rosemary was emblematic of remembrance, medieval physicians prescribed it to "strengthen the mind." They also pressed oil from rosemary leaves, stirred it with wine, and used the mixture to cure patients suffering from loss of speech, sore eyes, and skin diseases. The herb supposedly was a sure remedy for many other ills and was even credited with preventing baldness.

Centuries before the alchemists and doctors of the Middle Ages were compounding cosmetics and medicines from rosemary, the Greeks and Romans employed the herb to cure colds and were convinced that it stopped coughing and sneezing. They also used it in religious rites.

The early Christians not only burned rosemary as an incense in their churches but also linked the plant with the Virgin Mary. There is a charming legend concerning this herb which maintains that its blossoms were originally a dull white. But they were transformed into their present color after being touched by Mary's cape when she and the Infant Jesus hid from Herod's soldiers beneath a rosemary bush during the Flight into Egypt. In appreciation of its protection, the flowers of rosemary remained forever blue.

SAGE

There are approximately five hundred species of sage. Their range extends southward from the cool areas of both the Old and New Worlds to the warm temperate regions of both hemispheres. Botanists classify all the members of this large plant in the genus *Salvia*, a name they derived from the Latin *salvare* (to save). They chose *Salvia* because sage has been credited with valuable medicinal properties for centuries. This belief is illustrated by the ancient proverb: *"Cur moriatur homo, ciu salvia crescit in horto"*—Why should a man die who has sage in his garden?

Sage is a shrubby perennial and the majority of species have wrinkled gray-green foliage. However, the family includes plants that have purple, dark green, and variegated leaves. Similarly, while most fragrant varieties have the same characteristic odor, a few have a different scent. For example, pineapple sage (*Salvia splendens*) has the aroma of its namesake.

While lovers of flowers grow various species of sage for their blue, bright red, purple, and pinkish-blue blossoms, herb gardeners who raise culinary species usually plant the common sage (*Salvia officinalis*), or white sage (*Salvia officinalis alba*), which has white-mottled foliage. Of the two, the former is better for pot culture. It is also easily grown outdoors. The seeds sprout readily and a plant will last for years if moderately watered, given plenty of sunshine, and lightly mulched during the winter. However, sage has a tendency to become woody as it ages. Thus it is advisable to start new plants every two or three years. This is easily done by placing cuttings in damp sand and setting them out or potting them when they are well rooted.

Outdoors, *officinalis* should be spaced eighteen inches apart. Both garden and container-grown plants respond to pruning in the spring when the new leaves appear. When trimming sage,

54

Sage has been highly regarded as a medicinal plant for centuries, and few herbs are more extensively used for seasoning foods: garden sage, pineapple sage, golden sage, purple sage, tricolor sage (left to right).

be sure to cut off all dead twigs.

Occasionally picking a few leaves by hand during the first season will not harm garden sage. But none of the top growth—which bears the tenderest and most aromatic foliage before the faint purple flowers blossom—should be cut until the herb is at least eight inches tall. After the first year, two or three harvests can be gleaned.

Oil of sage is extensively employed in the perfume industry, but the herb's greatest use is to flavor food. This is nothing new. The Greek and Romans seasoned rich meats with sage. The Anglo-Saxons cooked fish with it; a manuscript dated 1393 mentions "pygges in swass Sawge" (pork in sage sauce), and many early cookbooks suggest flavoring pork with sage. This advice is followed by modern manufacturers of pork sausage. Sage is also used by makers of cheese and purveyors of prepared meats, and few culinary herbs are as commonly used by the average housewife.

Dedicated to Zeus by the Greeks, sage was not only a popular cooking herb in ancient times but also was used by Hippocrates and other early doctors who prescribed that the foliage be brewed into a tea.

Until tea from China was imported into Europe in the seventeenth century, sage tea—still considered an excellent "spring tonic" by many individuals—was a popular beverage throughout the continent. But whether drunk as a tea, stirred with wine, or baked in bread, sage was thought to "breed" blood, cure headaches, strengthen both the body and the mind, prevent aging, and provide protection from the plague.

Sage was also believed to cure epilepsy, fevers, laryngitis, and palsy. Perhaps the most unusual medicinal use of sage is found in Chaucer's *The Knight's Tale*, in which the poet tells how the herb saved the lives of warriors with "wounds and broken arms."

Even as English farmers suffering from chill and fevers were

56

doctoring themselves by eating only seven sage leaves for breakfast every morning for a week, the Iroquois Indians were drinking sage tea to cure stiff joints, colds, and colic. Meanwhile, Jicarilla Apache shamans prevented their patients from having nightmares by brushing their faces with sage, which they called "ghost medicine."

American folklore not only maintains that sage will cure rheumatism but also that it will whiten teeth when mixed with vinegar. It is also held in isolated rural areas of the United States that sage will keep away ants. However, few southern farmers still believe that an individual can insure winning a case in court if he writes the names of the twelve Apostles on sage leaves, places the leaves in his shoes, and wears them while testifying.

THYME

Most of the sixty varieties of thyme originated in northern Europe. All are woody-stemmed, small-leaved perennials, some growing upright, others trailing along the ground. While the more or less pungent foliage of all species can be used for cooking, it is garden thyme (*Thymis vulgaris*) that is most commonly raised for culinary purposes.

About a foot tall, with attractive gray-green foliage, this charming plant requires little care. It can be propagated from cuttings, but raising plants from seed is more satisfactory. Because the seed is tiny it is best handled by mixing it with sand and the combination should be thinly scattered and then pressed down with the palm of the hand.

Thyme demands considerable sunshine and well-drained, dry, sandy soil. Indoors, overwatering can be avoided by filling at least a third of its pot with crock. In the garden, thyme should be set out eighteen inches apart. Because thyme, like sage, becomes woody with age, new plants should be started every two years.

Once thyme is established, a few leaves can be picked from time to time. Large sprigs should be cut only just before a plant blossoms or while it is blooming. At the start of each growing season, potted thyme will respond to being cut back to two inches above the soil by sending out lush growth.

Because thyme has a strong flavor, it must be used with care. If this is done, its aromatic leaves impart a subtle seasoning to eggs, fish, meats, poultry, salads, sauces, soups, chowders, stuffing, and vegetables.

"Thyme" means incense. Long before the herb was used for seasoning the Greeks burned it in their temples. They also employed thyme as a funeral decoration and planted it on graves. During the Middle Ages, the floors of churches and baronial halls were covered with thyme during funerals as well as on festive occasions. But these customs did not deter anyone from cooking with thyme. Besides using the herb in their kitchen, the Romans grazed their sheep in fields of thyme so the animals' flesh would acquire the herb's flavor—a practice still carried out along the eastern Italian coast.

However, the main use of thyme in ancient days was to attract bees. Thyme honey—particularly that from Sicily—was considered superior to all other types because of its taste and scent. References to the fragrance of thyme and the flavor it imparted to honey are common in the writings of Horace, Virgil, and other classical poets. Nor have modern authors neglected thyme. However, few have praised it so highly as Kipling who described, "The wind-bit thyme that smells of dawn in Paradise."

The early Greeks and Romans dosed themselves with oil of thyme whenever they suffered from asthma, bronchitis, or a cold. They also rubbed the oil into their foreheads to prevent sleeplessness and to relieve headaches. Eighteenth-century physicians considered thyme a sure cure for "nervous cases" and nightmares.

58

*The delightful perfume of
thyme makes it one of the
most popular of herbs.*

A single plant of thyme in full bloom. The flowers are purple.

Dwarf thyme

Star-edged thyme

Modern medicine also compounds oil of thyme in various pharmaceutical preparations. But the manufacturers of these medicines no longer depend entirely on oil distilled from the herb. Chemists have learned to produce oil of thyme synthetically.

60

4
Herbal
Beauty Aids

Thyme

"And thou shall make it a perfume . . . ."

Today, few individuals soothe their hot tired feet by placing wilted horseradish leaves in their shoes. But other herbs are as widely used to refresh the body, cleanse and tone the skin, restore brightness to dull hair, and enhance face and hand lotions as they were in earlier days.

While herbal products can be purchased in the cosmetic departments of large stores where they are very popular, anyone who raises herbs can make many of them at home. It is not a difficult task. For example, there is no better rinse for dull hair than half an ounce of dried rosemary leaves steeped in a pint of boiling water for half an hour. Substitute sage for rosemary and the infusion will darken the color of hair.

Herbal beauty baths are also inexpensively and easily prepared. They may be scented with individual herbs—lavender, mint, rosemary, and thyme are excellent choices—or with a combination of favorite fragrances. If dried leaves are used, merely place them in a small square of muslin or cheesecloth tied tightly to form a bag. Fresh foliage should be bruised slightly before bagging to release its aroma. The sachet can either be soaked in a quart of boiling water for fifteen minutes and the scented liquid poured into the bath or it can be dropped directly into the tub.

61

Since the days of the Pharaohs, camomile has been used to reduce swellings. The herb is also made into a tea and employed to scent cosmetics.

Ordinary rubbing alcohol can be transformed into a stimulating and refreshing herbal lotion. Fill a pint jar one-quarter full of aromatic foliage and pour alcohol over it to within an inch of the top. Seal the container tightly so that it can be shaken occasionally without spillage and let it stand for two weeks at room temperature. Finally, filter the liquid and rebottle. While a drop or two of pure food coloring will not make the lotion more efficacious, the addition will enhance its appearance.

Because dried lavender blossoms retain their delightful odor for years, they have long been used to perfume stored linens. Lavender, the symbol of purity, is also employed to scent bath salts, soap, and toilet water.

Herbs and vinegar combine into an excellent skin refresher and a hair rinse. There are several recipes for these slightly astringent beauty aids, all of which are known as "herbal vinegar." Some recipes call for an ounce each of mint, rosemary, and sage leaves; others for only an ounce of any of these herbs. Whether a single herb or several are employed, the dried foliage should stand in four ounces of white vinegar for two weeks under refrigeration, then be strained before rebottling.

If you save fancy bottles and jars from commercial products, you can make unusual gifts from your favorite herbal creations. A gay ribbon, decoupage, or a sprig or two of dried flowers can dress up your product, and you may also find these items salable at flea markets or garage sales.

There are dozens of other herbal cosmetics one can manufacture. Directions for compounding them can be found in many of the books dealing with herb cookery available in most public libraries. However, it is far more fun to devise personal formulas. But while you are busy with mortar, pestle, filter paper, and dried and fresh herb leaves, watch out for witches —they hate beauty.

Actually, there's no need to be concerned that a witch will appear while you're making a potpourri, sachet, bath blend, or lotion. Just remember to hang a sprig of dill above your worktable and it will keep witches and all other evil folk away!

Medieval doctors would be amazed to see the techniques employed by modern industry to distil the essential oils of herbs for cosmetics, medicines, and cooking.

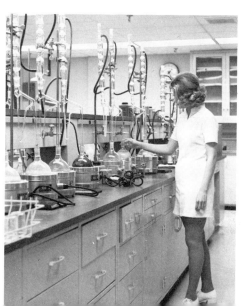

Index